This book belongs to

A catalogue record for this book is available from the British Library
Published by Ladybird Books Ltd.
A Penguin Company
80 Strand, London, WC2R 0RL, England
Penguin Books Australia Ltd, 250 Camberwell Road,
Camberwell, Victoria 3124, Australia
New York, Canada, India, New Zealand, South Africa

001 - 10 9 8 7 6 5 4 3 2 1

This edition published 2011

Planned and produced by Ventura Publishing Ltd
80 Strand, London WC2R 0RL

ISBN 978-0-72326-758-4

Printed in China

Spot's
Camping Trip

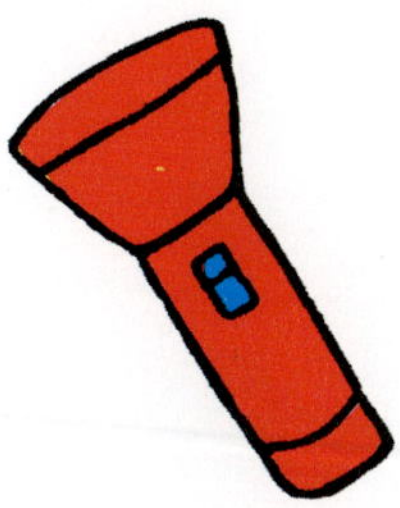

Eric Hill

One rainy morning, Spot looked out of the window in Sally's room.
"Can I go out to play, Mum?" he asked.

"I think it's too wet to play outdoors today," said Mum.
"Then can Steve and Helen come here to play?" Spot asked.
"Of course," said Mum. "Let's call them now."

A few minutes later, Steve and Helen were at the door. Both of them were very wet.

Spot helped his friends hang up their raincoats and put away their dripping umbrellas and wellies.

Spot and his friends went to Spot's room. They took all the toys out of the toy chest. They took all the games down from the shelf. But nobody could decide what to play with.

Suddenly Spot had an idea. "I know," he said. "Let's go camping!"

"But it's wet outside," said Helen. "Yes," said Steve. "How can we go camping in the rain?"
"I'll show you," said Spot, who was already rushing out of the door with a blanket. "Follow me – and bring the torch."

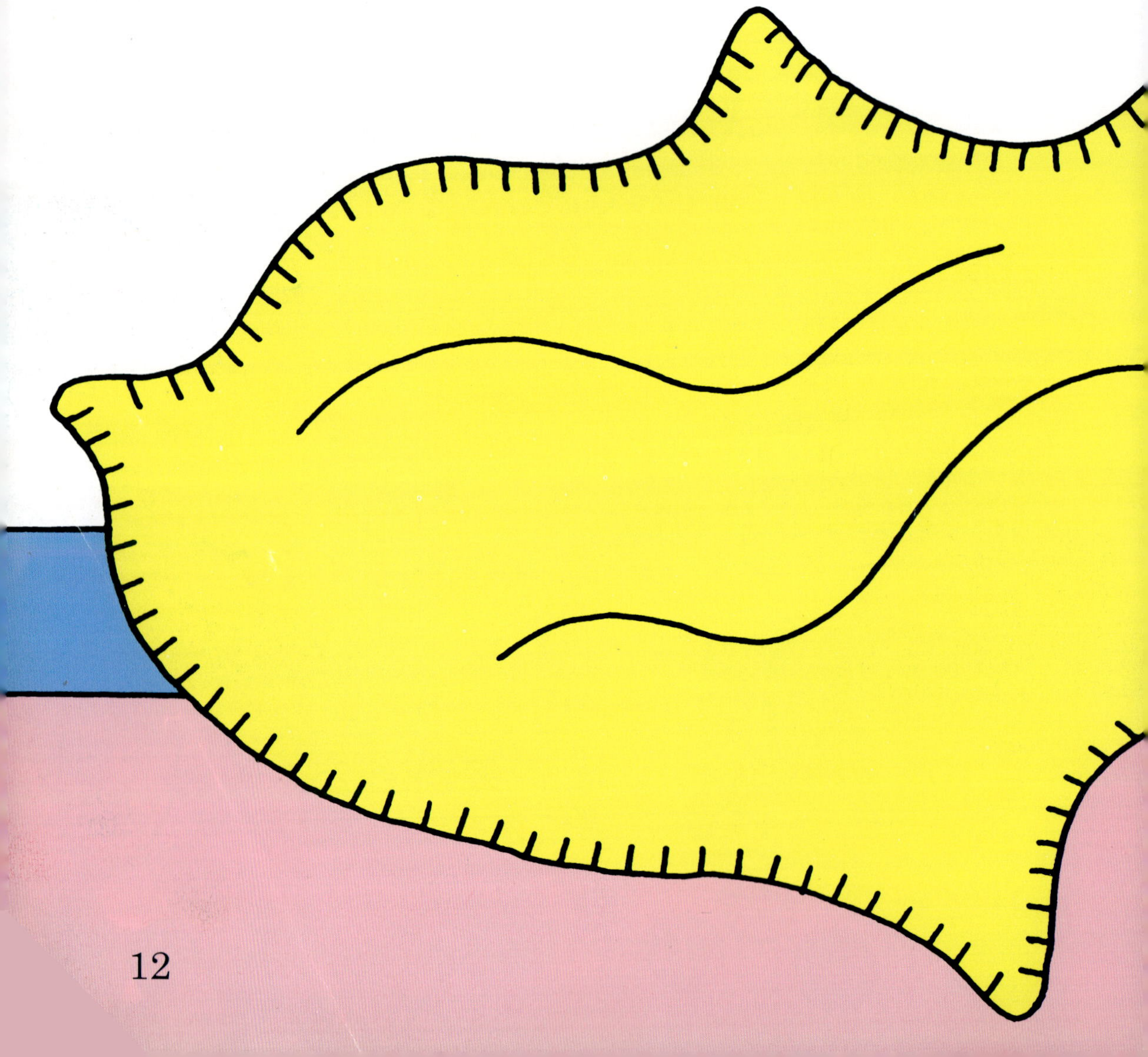

Spot pulled some chairs out into the middle of the kitchen. He put the blanket over them.

“This will be our tent,” he said.
“We can pretend we’re in
the woods.”
“The table can be the trees!”
said Helen.

Spot and Steve crawled into the tent.
"It's just like a real tent," said Steve. "And look! We can make shadows with the torch."

Steve and Spot had fun making lots of different shadows. Spot made a shadow that looked like a mouse. Steve made a shadow that looked like a rabbit.

All at once, Spot and Steve realised that Helen wasn't there. "Where can she be?" Spot wondered.

"I don't know," said Steve.
"But what's that noise?"
There was a strange growling
coming from outside the tent!

Steve and Spot peeped out to see what the noise was.
"It's me!" said Helen.
"I'm pretending to be a bear!"
Spot and Steve laughed.

“I thought it was my tummy growling,” said Spot, “because I’m hungry. If we’re camping, we should have a picnic.”

"Did you say picnic?" said a voice. It was Spot's mum – bringing a picnic basket filled with yummy food.

"Thanks, Mum," said Spot. "You're just in time. I think my tummy really was starting to sound like a very big, angry bear!"

Spot, Steve and Helen shared all the sandwiches and fruit. And there was a surprise at the bottom of the picnic basket.

“Biscuits!” said Helen.
“My favourites,” said Spot.
“This is a perfect picnic.”

"This is so much fun," said Steve.
"I hope it never stops raining."
"But it has stopped," said Helen.
The sun was shining through the kitchen window – and there was a beautiful rainbow in the sky.

"Great!" said Spot, gathering up the blanket. "Now we can go camping for real."
"In the woods?" asked Steve.
"No," said Spot, "In the garden. And this time I'm going to be the bear!"

“Hooray!” they all cried, rushing outside for their next camping adventure.